I0117425

Lev Tolstoy

Epilogue to Drozhzhin's Life and Death

Lev Tolstoy

Epilogue to Drozhzhin's Life and Death

ISBN/EAN: 9783337321055

Printed in Europe, USA, Canada, Australia, Japan

Cover: Foto ©Thomas Meinert / pixelio.de

More available books at **www.hansebooks.com**

Epilogue to Drózhzhin's Life and Death

Lev Tolstoy

Epilogue to Drózhzhin's Life and Death by Lev Tolstoy

Even Moses in his commandments, which were given to men five thousand years ago, proclaimed the commandment, "Thou shalt not kill." The same was preached by all the prophets; the same was preached by the sages and teachers of the whole world; the same was preached by Christ, who forbade men to commit not only murder, but also everything that may lead to it – all irritation and anger against a brother. The same is written in the heart of every man so clearly that there is no act that is more loathsome to the whole being of an uncorrupted man than the murder of one's fellow man.

And yet, despite the fact that this law of God was clearly revealed to us by Moses, by the prophets, and by Christ, and that it is so indelibly written in our hearts that there cannot be the slightest doubt of its being obligatory for us, this law is not recognized in our world. Instead, the very opposite law is recognized, that of the obligation for every man of our time to enter military service, that is, to join the ranks of murderers, to swear to be ready to commit murder, to learn the art of killing, and actually to kill his fellow man when that is demanded of him.
(In countries where there is no compulsory military service, the law of God and of conscience about not killing is also violated by all their citizens, though not so obviously. The hiring, enlisting, and maintaining of armies, with the money consciously paid by all the citizens for the business of murder, which they all consider to be indispensable, is just as much a consent to killing and a cooperation with it as the personal participation in military service.)

In pagan times, the Christians were commanded in words to renounce Christ and God, and as a sign of the renunciation to bring sacrifices to the pagan gods. But now, in our time, the Christians are commanded not only to renounce Christ and God by bringing sacrifices to pagan gods (a person may sacrifice to pagan gods, while remaining a Christian at heart), but also by committing an act which is unquestionably most contrary to Christ and to

God and which is forbidden by Christ and by God: to swear to be ready to commit murder, to prepare himself for murder, and frequently to commit murder itself.

And as formerly there were found men who refused to worship pagan gods, and for their loyalty to Christ and God sacrificed their lives, so there have been men who have not renounced Christ and God, who have not consented to take an oath that they would be ready to commit murder, who did not join the ranks of murderers, and who for this loyalty have perished in the most terrible sufferings, as was the case with Drózhzhin, whose life is described in this book. In former times the martyrs of Christianity, who were considered half-witted and strange, who perished because they did not wish to renounce Christ, destroyed the pagan world by their loyalty to Christ alone and opened a path for Christianity. So now, people like Drózhzhin, who are considered to be madmen and fanatics, who prefer sufferings and death to transgressing God's law, by their very loyalty to the law destroy the existing cruel order more surely than do the revolutions. They reveal to men the new joyful condition of universal brotherhood, of the kingdom of God, which was proclaimed by the prophets, and the foundations of which were laid eighteen hundred years ago by Christ.

But such men as Drózhzhin, who now refuse to renounce God and Christ, by their activity not only contribute to the establishment of that kingdom of God which the prophets predicted, but by their example indicate the one unquestionable road by which this kingdom of God may be attained and all that may be destroyed which interferes with its establishment. The difference between the ancient martyrs of Christianity and those of the present time consists only in this: then it was the pagans who demanded pagan acts from the Christians, while now it is not pagans, but Christians, or at least those who call themselves so, that are demanding from Christians the most terrible pagan acts, such as the pagans did not ask for – murder. Then paganism found its strength in ignorance because it did not know and did not understand Christianity, while now the cruelty of the so-called Christianity is based on conscious deception. To free Christianity from violence then it was necessary to convince the pagans of the truth of Christianity, but that was for the most part impossible to do. Julian the Apostate and many of the best men of the time were sincerely convinced that paganism was enlightened and good, and Christianity was darkness, ignorance, and evil. But to free Christianity now from violence and cruelty, it is necessary to arraign the deception of the false Christianity. This deception unanswerably arraigns itself through one simple, imperturbable profession of the truth, which inevitably provokes the so-called Christian powers to the exercise of violence, to tortures, and to the killing of Christians for observing precisely what they themselves profess.

Formerly, a Christian, in refusing to worship the pagan gods, said to the pagans, "I reject your faith. I am a Christian, and I cannot and will not serve your gods, but will serve the one true God and His son Jesus Christ." The pagan powers punished him because he professed a religion that they considered to be false and harmful, and his punishment had no contradiction in itself and did not undermine paganism, in the name of which he was punished. But now a Christian who refuses to commit murder no longer makes his confession to pagans, but to men who call themselves Christians. And if he says, "I am a Christian, and I cannot and will not fulfill any demands for committing murder, which are contrary to the Christian law," he can no longer be told, as he was formerly told by the pagans, "You are professing a false and harmful teaching." Instead, he is told, "We are also Christians, but you do not correctly understand Christianity when you assert that a Christian may not kill. A Christian can and must kill, when he is commanded to do so by someone who at a given moment is considered to be his chief. And because you do not agree with this, that a Christian must not love his enemies, and must kill all those whom he is commanded to kill, we, the Christians, who profess the law of humility, love, and forgiveness, punish you."

It turns out that the powers which recognize themselves as being Christian, at every such a conflict with men who refuse to commit murder, are compelled in the most obvious and solemn manner to renounce that Christianity and moral law on which alone their power is based. Besides, unfortunately for the false powers, and fortunately for all humanity, the conditions of military service have of late become quite different from what they were before, and so the demands of the authorities have become even more obviously non-

Christian, and the refusals to fulfill their demands have arraigned Christianity even more.

Formerly, hardly one man in a hundred was called to do military service, and the government was in a position to assume that men of a lower stage of morality took to military service, men for whom military service did not present anything contrary to their Christian conscience, as was partly the case when men were put in the army for a punishment. When at that time a man, who by his moral qualities could not be a murderer, was called to do military service, such a case was unfortunate and exceptional.

But now, when everybody has to do military service, the best men, those who are most Christian in their thoughts and who are far removed from the possibility of taking part in murder, must all recognize themselves as being murderers and apostates from God. Formerly, the hired army of the ruler was formed by specially chosen, very coarse, non- Christian, and ignorant men, or volunteers and mercenaries. Formerly, only a few men read the Gospel and men did not know its spirit, but only believed in what the priest told them. Formerly, only the rarest people, who were peculiarly fanatical in spirit, the sectarians, considered military service to be a sin and refused to take part in it. But now there is not a man in any Christian state who is not obliged consciously, by means of his money, and in most countries of Europe directly, to take part in the preparations for murder or in the murders themselves. Now nearly all men know the Gospel and the spirit of Christ's teaching. All know that the priests are bribed deceivers and none but the most ignorant men believe in them. Now it is not merely the sectarians, but also men who do not profess any special dogmas, cultured men, free thinkers, who refuse to do military service, and they do not refuse merely for their own sake, but openly and outspokenly say to all men that murder is not compatible with any profession of Christianity. And so, one such refusal to do military service like Drózhzhin's, which is sustained in spite of tortures and death – one such refusal shakes the whole enormous structure of violence, which is built on a lie, and threatens its destruction.

Governments have a terrible power in their hands, and it is not merely a material power – a vast amount of money, institutions, wealth, submissive officials, the clergy, and the army – but also vast spiritual powers of influencing men that are in the hands of the government. It can, if not bribe, at least crush and destroy all those who are opposed to it. A bribed clergy preaches militarism in the churches. Bribed authors write books that justify militarism. In the schools, both the higher and the lower, they have introduced the obligatory instruction of deceptive catechisms, in which children are impressed with the idea that it is not only allowable, but even obligatory, to kill in war and after a trial. All those who enter the army are compelled to take an oath. Everything that could reveal the deception is strictly prohibited and punished, and the most terrible punishments are imposed upon men who do not fulfill the demands of serving in the army – that is, of killing.

And, strange to say, all that enormous, mighty mass of men, which is vested with all the force of human power, trembles, hides itself, feeling its guilt, is shaken to its foundation, and is ready at any moment to go to pieces and turn to dust at the appearance of one man, like Drózhzhin, who does not yield to human demands, but obeys the demands of God and professes them openly.

In our time such men as Drózhzhin do not stand alone; there are thousands, tens of thousands of them. Their number and, above all else, their importance are growing with every year and every hour. In Russia we know tens of thousands of men who have refused to swear allegiance to the new czar, and who recognize military service to be murder, which is incompatible not only with Christianity, but even with the lowest demands of honor, justice, and morality. We know such men in all European countries. We know of the Nazarenes, who appeared less than fifty years ago in Austria and Serbia and who from a few hundred have grown to be more than thirty thousand strong, and who, in spite of all kinds of persecution, have refused to take part in military service. We have learned lately of a highly cultured surgeon of the army, who refused to do military service because he considered it contrary to his conscience to serve such an institution as is the army, which is intended only for doing violence to men and killing them. But it is not important that there are many of them and that they are growing more and more. What is important is that the one true path has been found along which humanity will undoubtedly arrive at its liberation from evil, which has fettered it. On that path to liberation nothing and nobody can now stop it, because no efforts are wanted for the destruction of evil – it disperses of its own accord and melts like wax in the fire. All that is needed is a nonparticipation in it. In order to stop taking part in this evil, from which we suffer, no special mental or bodily efforts are needed. All that is needed is to abandon oneself to one's nature, and to be good and true before God and oneself.

"You want me to become a murderer, but I cannot do so, and neither God nor my conscience permit me to do so. And so do with me what you please, but I will neither kill, nor prepare myself for murder, nor be an accomplice in it." And this simple answer, which every man must inevitably make because it arises from the consciousness of the men of our time, destroys all that evil of violence that has weighed heavily on the world for so long a time.

They say that in Holy Scripture it says, "Everyone must submit himself to the governing authorities, for there is no authority except that which God has established. The authorities that exist have been established by God. Consequently, he who rebels against the authority is rebelling against what God has instituted, and those who do so will bring judgment on themselves. For rulers hold no terror for those who do right, but for those who do wrong. Do you want to be free from fear of the one in authority? Then do what is right and he will commend you, for he is God's servant to do you good. But if you do wrong, be afraid, for he does not bear the sword for nothing. He is God's servant, an agent of wrath to bring punishment on the wrongdoer. Therefore, it is necessary to submit to the authorities, not only because of possible punishment, but also because of conscience. This is also why you pay taxes, for the authorities are God's servants, who give their full time to governing. Give everyone what you owe him: if you owe taxes, pay taxes; if revenue, then revenue; if respect, then respect; if honor, then honor." (Romans 13:1-7) Consequently, it is necessary to submit to the powers. But to say nothing of this, that the same politic Paul, who told the Romans that it is necessary to obey the authorities, told the Ephesians something quite different: "Finally, be strong in the Lord and in his mighty power. Put on the full armor of God so that you can take your stand against the devil's schemes. For our struggle is not against flesh and blood, but against the rulers, against the authorities, against the powers of this dark world and against the spiritual forces of evil in the heavenly realms." (Ephesians 6:10-12)

Paul's words to the Romans about obeying the powers that be can in no way be harmonized with Christ's own teaching, the whole meaning of which consists in the liberation of men from the power of the world and their submission to the power of God. "If the world hates you, keep in mind that it hated me first." (John 15:18) "If they persecuted me, they will persecute you also." (John 15:20) "If you belonged to the world, it would love you as its own. As it is, you do not belong to the world, but I have chosen you out of the world. That is why the world hates you." (John 15:19) "On my account you will be brought before governors and kings as witnesses to them and to the Gentiles." (Matthew 10:18, Mark 13:9) "All men will hate you because of me." (Matthew 10:22) "They will lay hands on you and persecute you. They will deliver you to synagogues and prisons, and you will be brought before kings and governors, and all on account of my name." (Luke 21:12) "A time is coming when anyone who kills you will think he is offering a service to God. They will do such things because they have not known the Father or me. I have told you this, so that when the time comes you will remember that I warned you." (John 16:2-4) "So do not be afraid of them. There is nothing concealed that will not be disclosed, or hidden that will not be made known." (Matthew 10:26) "Do not be afraid of those who kill the body but cannot kill the soul. Rather, be afraid of the One who can destroy both soul and body in hell." (Matthew 10:28) "The prince of this world now stands condemned." (John 16:11) "But take heart! I have overcome the world." (John 16:33)

Christ's whole teaching is an indication of the path of liberation from the power of the world, and Christ, when He was Himself persecuted, reminded His disciples that, if they would be true to His teaching, the world would persecute them, and advised them to have courage and not be afraid of their persecutors. He not only taught them this in words, but also with His whole life and relationship to the powers He gave them an example of how those must act who wish to follow Him. Christ not only did not obey the powers, but all the time kept arraigning them. He arraigned the Pharisees for violating God's law with their human traditions; He arraigned them for falsely observing the Sabbath and for falsely sacrificing in the temple; He arraigned them for their hypocrisy and cruelty; He arraigned the cities of Korazin,

Bethsaida, and Capernaum; He arraigned Jerusalem and predicted its ruin.

In reply to the question as to whether He shall give the established tax upon entering Capernaum, He says distinctly that the sons, that is, His disciples, are free from every tax and are not obliged to pay it, and only not to tempt the collectors of the taxes, not to provoke them to commit the sin of violence, He orders His disciples to give that stater, which is accidentally found in the fish, and which does not belong to any one and is not taken from any one. But in reply to the cunning question as to whether the tribute is to be paid to Caesar, He says, "Give to Caesar what is Caesar's, and to God what is God's," that is, give to Caesar what belongs to him and is made by him – the coin – and to God give what is made by God and is implanted in you – your soul, your conscience. Give this to no one but God, and so do not do for Caesar what is forbidden by God. And this answer surprises all by its boldness – and at the same time by its unanswerableness.
(The striking misinterpretation of the words, "Give to Caesar what is Caesar's," as signify the necessity of obeying Caesar indicates not only the complete misunderstanding of Christ's teaching, but also a complete unwillingness to understand it. In the first place, there is no mention there of obedience. In the second place, if Christ recognized the obligation of paying tribute, and also of obedience, He would have said directly, "Yes, it should be paid." Instead He says, "Give to Caesar what is his – that is, the money – and give your life to God." With these latter words He not only does not encourage any obedience to power, but, on the contrary, points out that in everything that belongs to God it is not right to obey Caesar.)

When Christ is brought before Pilate, as a mutineer who has been perverting the nation and forbidding to give tribute to Caesar (Luke 23:2), He, after saying what He found necessary to say, surprises and provokes all the chiefs with this: He pays no attention and makes no reply to any of their questions.

For this arraignment of power and disobedience to it, Christ is sentenced and crucified. The whole story of Christ's suffering and death is nothing but the story of those calamities to which every man will inevitably be subjected, if he follows Christ's example of obedience to God and not to the powers of the world. Suddenly we are assured that the whole of Christ's teaching must not only be corrected, but even be abolished in consequence of the thoughtless and cunning words which Paul wrote to the Romans.

But Paul's words contradict Christ's teaching and life with all the desire to obey the powers, as Paul commands us to do, not only from fear, but also from conviction, and in our time such an obedience has become absolutely impossible.

To say nothing of the inner contradiction between Christianity and the obedience to the powers, such obedience to the powers, not from fear, but from conviction, has become impossible in our day. This is because, in consequence of the universal diffusion of enlightenment, the power, as something worthy of respect, something exalted, and, above all, something definite and whole, has been completely destroyed in our time, and there is no possibility of reestablishing it.

It was all very well, not only from fear, but also from conviction, to obey the power when the men under the power saw what the Romans saw in it: the emperor-god. The Chinese see the sun of heaven in their emperor. Men in the Middle Ages, and even down to the Revolution, saw the kings and emperors as divinely anointed men. Until lately in Russia, the masses saw in the czar an earthly god. Czars, kings, and emperors were not represented except in majestic situations, doing wise and great things. But it is quite different today when, in spite of all the efforts of the powers, their friends, and even the subjects themselves to reestablish awe for the power, enlightenment, history, experience, and communication of men among themselves have destroyed this awe. It is as impossible to reestablish it as it is in the spring to reestablish the melted snow, and as impossible to construct anything firm upon it as it is to travel in a sleigh over a widely spreading river, from which the ice has disappeared.

It cannot be otherwise, since now all men, with the exception of the coarsest and most uncultured of men, whose number is growing less and less, know what immoral persons were Louis XI, Elizabeth of England, John IV, Catherine, Napoleon, and Nicholas I. These people ruled and decided the fates of millions, and did not rule thanks to some sacred, invariable law, as people used to think formerly, but only because they were able by means of all kinds of deceptions, by cunning, and by rascalities so to strengthen their power that it was impossible to dethrone, kill, or drive them away, as was done in the case of Charles I, Louis XVI, Maximilian of Mexico, Louis Philippe, and others.

It cannot be otherwise, since all men know that even the kings and emperors who rule at the present time are not some special, holy, great, wise people, who are interested in the good of their nations. On the contrary, for the most part they are very badly educated, ignorant, vainglorious, immoral, and frequently very stupid and bad men who are always corrupted by luxury and flattery. They are not at all interested in the good of their subjects, but in their own personal affairs, and are, above all else, without cessation concerned in maintaining their tottering power, which is upheld only by means of cunning and deception.

Not only do men now see the material of which their rulers are made, who formerly presented themselves to them as special beings, and not only have men peeped behind the curtain so that it is impossible to reconstruct the old illusion, they also see and know that it is not really these rulers who rule. In constitutional states, the members of the parliaments, the ministers who attain their positions by means of intrigues and bribes, and in unconstitutional countries, the wives, paramours, favorites, flatterers, and all kinds of parasitic accomplices are the ones who truly rule.

How can a man respect the power and obey it, not from fear, but from conviction, when he knows that this power is not something that exists separately from him, but is the product of men's intrigues and cunning, and constantly passes from one person to another? Knowing this, a man can not only not obey the power from conviction, but cannot even help trying to destroy the existing power and to become it himself, making his way into power, and seizing as much of it as he can. And this is actually taking place.

The power of which Paul spoke, the power that one can obey from conviction, has outlived its day. It no longer exists. It has melted like the ice and it will not support anything. What formerly was a solid surface of the river is now liquid, and in order to journey over it we do not need a sleigh and horses, but a boat and oars. Even so, the composition of life has so completely changed, as the result of education, that the power, in the sense in which it used to be understood, has no longer any place in our world, and all there is left is rude violence and deception. But it is impossible to obey violence and deception "not from fear, but from conviction."

"But how can we help obeying the powers? If we do not obey the powers, terrible calamities will occur, and bad men will torment, oppress, and kill the good."

I say myself, "How can we help but obey the power? How can we make up our minds not to obey the power, the one unquestionable power, from which we shall never get away, under which we always are, and the demands of which we know incontestably and unerringly?" They say, "How can we make up our minds not to obey the powers?"

What powers? In the time of Catherine, when Pugachév rebelled, half the people swore allegiance to Pugachév and were under his power. Well, what power had to be obeyed? Catherine's or Pugachév's? And again, who was to be obeyed in the time of the same Catherine, who usurped the power from her husband, the czar, to whom people had sworn allegiance? Was it Peter III or Catherine?

Not one Russian czar, from Peter I to Nicholas I included, assumed the throne in such a way that it was clear what power was to be obeyed. Who was to be obeyed, Peter I or Sophia, or John, Peter's elder brother? Sophia had just as much right to the throne, and the proof of it is that, after her, women ruled who had even less right to it: the two Catherines, Anna, and Elizabeth. Whose power was to be obeyed after Peter, when some courtiers raised a soldier woman to the throne, the paramour of Ménshikov, Sheremétev, and Peter – Catherine I – and then Peter II, and then Anna and Elizabeth, and finally Catherine II? She had no more right to the throne than had Pugachév, since during her reign the legitimate heir, John, was kept in prison and was killed by her order, and there was another unquestionably legitimate heir, Paul, who was of age. And whose power had to be obeyed, Paul's or

Alexander's, at the time that the conspirators, who killed Paul, were just getting ready to kill him? And whose power had to be obeyed, Constantino's or Nicholas's, when Nicholas took the power away from Constantino? All history is the history of the struggle of one power against another, not only in Russia, but also in all the other countries.

More than this – must we, not in time of civil war and the dethronement of one set of rulers and the substitution of another set in their place, but in the most peaceful times, obey Arakchéev, who seized the power, or must we try to overthrow him and convince the czar of the worthlessness of his ministers? Not the supreme power, but its servants control men. Must we obey these servants, when their demands are obviously bad and detrimental?

Thus, no matter how much we may desire to obey the power, we cannot do so, because there is not one definite earthly power, but all the powers of the earth waver, change, and fight among themselves. What power is the real one, and when is it real? And so, what power is to be obeyed?

But not only is the power which demands obedience doubtful, and we cannot know whether it is the real one or not – it also demands of us acts that are not indifferent and harmless. It does not demand acts such as building a pyramid, a temple, or a castle, or even serving the mighty of this earth and satisfying their lusts and their luxury. That would still be possible to do. Instead, this doubtful power demands of us that we should commit the most terrible act for a man: murder, the preparation for it, and the acknowledgment of our readiness for it. It demands an act that is obviously prohibited by God, and which, therefore, causes our souls to perish. Is it possible that I must, out of obedience to this human, accidental, wavering, discordant power, forget the demands of that one divine power, which is so clearly and so indubitably known to me, and cause my soul to perish?

"We cannot help obeying the power."

"Yes, we cannot help obeying the power," I myself say, "only it is not the power of an emperor, king, president, parliament, and the chiefs chosen by them, whom I do not know and with whom I have nothing in common, but the power of God whom I know, with whom I live, from whom I received my soul, and to whom I shall return it tomorrow, if not today." I am told, "There will be calamities if we are not going to obey the power." And they tell the actual truth if by power they mean the real power, and not the human deception that is called power. There are those calamities, and they are terrible, horrible calamities, through which we are passing now, for the very reason that we do not obey the one unquestionable power of God, which was clearly revealed to us in Scripture and in our hearts.

We say, "Our calamities consist in the rich and the idle growing richer, and the poor and the laboring people growing poorer. The masses are deprived of land, and so are compelled to do convict labor in the factories that manufacture articles that they do not use. The masses are made drunk on whiskey, which the government sells to them. Young men go into the army, become corrupted, spread diseases, and are made unfit for a simple life of labor. The rich sit in judgment in the courts, while the poor sit in prisons. The masses are stultified in the schools and churches, and officials and the clergy are rewarded for this by means of the money taken from the masses. All the popular forces, men, and money are used for war and the army, and this army is in the hands of the rulers, who by means of this army crush everything that is not in harmony with their advantage."

These calamities are terrible, but from where do they come? On what are they based? Only on this: that men do not obey the one true power and its law, which is written in their hearts, but obey invented human statutes that they call the law. If men obeyed this one true power of God and His law, they would not take upon themselves the obligation to kill their like, would not enter the army, and would not give money for the hire and support of an army. If there were no army, there would not be all those cruelties and all that injustice, which it supports. Only by means of an army is it possible to establish and maintain such an order that all the land is in the hands of those who do not work it, and those who work are deprived of it. Only by means of an army is it possible to take away the labors of the poor and give them to the rich. Only by means of an army is it possible purposely to stupefy the masses and deprive them of the possibility of real enlightenment. All that is supported by means of an army. But the army consists of soldiers, and we are the soldiers. If there were no soldiers, there would not be anything of the kind.

The condition of men is now such that nothing can change it but obedience to the true power, and not to the false power.

"But this new condition without an army, without a government, will be many times worse than the one we are in now," we are told. "Worse for whom?" I ask. "For those who now rule, for one percent of the whole nation? For that part of the nation, of course, it will be worse, but not for all the mass of working people, who are deprived of the land and of the products of their labor, for the simple reason that for this ninety-nine percent of the people the condition cannot be worse than it now is."

And by what right do we assume that the condition of men will become worse, if they obey the law of not committing murder, which is revealed to them by God and is implanted in their hearts? To say that everything in this world will get worse, if the men in it follow the law that God gave them for life in this world, is the same as though we should say that it will be worse, if men are going to use a machine that is given to them, not according to their arbitrary will, but according to the instruction regarding the use of the machine, which is given them by him who invented and constructed the machine.

There was a time when humanity lived like wild beasts, and everybody took for himself in life everything that he could, taking away from others what he wanted, and killing and annihilating his neighbors. Then there came a time when men united into societies and states and began to establish themselves as nations, defending themselves against other nations. Men became less similar to beasts but still considered it not only possible, but even indispensable and proper to kill their domestic and foreign enemies. Now the time is at hand and is already here when men, according to Christ's words, are entering into the new condition of the brotherhood of all men, into that new condition that was long ago predicted by the prophets, when all men shall be taught by God, shall forget how to fight, shall forge the swords into ploughshares and the spears into pruning-hooks, and there will come the kingdom of God, the kingdom of union and of peace. This condition was predicted by the prophets, but Christ's teaching showed how and through what it could be implemented: through brotherly union, one of the first manifestations of which must be the abolition of violence. The necessity of the destruction of violence is already recognized by men, and so this condition will arrive as inevitably as formerly the political condition followed after the savage state.

Humanity in our time is in the birth pangs of this nascent kingdom of God, and this labor will inevitably end in birth. But the arrival of this new life will not take place of its own accord. It depends on us. We must do it all. The kingdom of God is within us.

In order to produce this kingdom of God within us, we do not need, I repeat, any special mental or physical conditions. We need only be what we are, what God made us: rational and, above all, good beings, who follow the voice of our conscience.

"But that is where the trouble is. Men are neither rational nor good beings." I already hear the voices of those men who, to have the right to be bad, assert that the whole human race is bad and that this is not merely an experimental, but also a divine, revealed, religious truth. "Men are all evil and irrational," they assert, "and so it is necessary for the rational and good men to maintain order."

But if all men are irrational and bad, from where shall we take the rational and the good? And if there are such, how are we going to tell them? And if we can tell them, by what means shall we (who are those "we" going to be?) put them at the head of other men? But even if we shall be able to put these special, rational, and good men at the head of the others, will not these rational and good men stop being such if they are going to exert violence and punish the irrational and the bad? And, above all else, you say that, in order to keep some thieves, pillagers, and murderers from violating and killing men, you are going to establish courts, a police, and an army, which will constantly violate and kill men, and whose duty will consist in nothing else, and into these institutions you will draw all men. But in such a case you are putting in the place of a small and assumed evil another that is greater, a universal and a certain evil. In order to defend ourselves against some imaginary murderers, you compel all men certainly to become murderers. And so I repeat that for the realization of a brotherly relationship among men we need no special efforts, no mental or bodily efforts, but need only be what God made us – rational and good beings – and act in conformity with these characteristics.

It is not for every one of us to bear all the trials that Drózhzhin endured (although, if this shall be our fate, may God help us to bear it all without being false to Him), but whether we want it or not – even if we live in a country where there is no military duty or we are not called upon to perform such duty – everyone is called in one way or another to subject himself to the same trial and, whether he wills so or not, to stand on the side of the oppressors or himself to become an oppressor, or to stand on the side of the oppressed, helping them to bear their trials, or to undergo them himself. Every one of us, even if we do not take any direct part in the persecutions against these new martyrs, as do the emperors, ministers, governors, and judges, who sign the decrees for the torturing of these martyrs, or as tormentors such as jailers, guards, and executioners do still more directly themselves – every one of us nonetheless has to take an active part in these affairs by means of those opinions which we pass upon them in print, in letters, and in conversations. Frequently we, out of laziness, do not reflect on the significance of such a phenomenon, only because we do not wish to impair our peace by a lively representation of what is being suffered by those men who on account of their truthfulness, sincerity, and love of men are pining away in prisons and in places of deportation. We repeat, without thinking of what we are saying, opinions that we have heard or read elsewhere. "What is to be done? It serves them right. They are harmful fanatics, and the government must suppress such attempts." We say these and similar words, which support the persecutors and increase the sufferings of the persecuted. We will think ten times about an act of ours, about the disbursement of a certain sum or about the destruction or construction of a house, but it seems of so little consequence to say a few words that we generally speak without thinking. And yet, speech is the most significant of all the acts that we can perform. Public opinion is composed from what is said, and public opinion more than all the kings and sovereigns rules all the affairs of men. And so every opinion of ours, concerning acts such as Drózhzhin's act, may be a work of God that contributes to the realization of the kingdom of God and the brotherhood of men, and that helps those advanced men who give their lives for its realization. Or, it may be a work that is hostile to God, that works against Him, and that contributes to the torments of those men who abandon themselves to His service.

Drózhzhin tells in his diary of one such cruel effect produced upon him by frivolous words that were hostile to God. He tells how in the first period of his incarceration when he, in spite of all his physical sufferings and all his humiliation, continued to experience joyous peace in the consciousness that he had done what he ought to have done, he was affected by a letter from a friend of his, a revolutionist, who, out of love for him, tried to persuade him to have pity on himself, to recant, and to do the will of the authorities – to take the oath and serve. Apparently this young man, who had the spirit of a revolutionist and according to the customary code of the revolutionists admitted as a principle that the end justifies the means and that all kinds of compromises with his conscience were allowable, absolutely failed to understand those religious sentiments which guided Drózhzhin, and so had written him frivolously asking him not to throw away his life, which was a useful tool for the revolution, and to fulfill all the demands of the authorities. These words, it would seem, ought not to have had any special significance, and yet Drózhzhin writes that these words deprived him of his peace and that he fell ill in consequence of them.

This is quite comprehensible. All men who move humanity forward and who are the first and foremost to step out on the path on which all men will soon walk, do not come out on this path lightly, but always with suffering and with an internal struggle. An inner voice draws them onto the new path, and all their attachments and the traditions of weakness draw them back. In such moments of unstable balance every word of support or, on the contrary, of retardation has an enormous importance.

The strongest man can be pulled over by a child, when this man is straining all his strength in order to move a burden that is above his strength.

Drózhzhin experienced terrible despair from these apparently unimportant words of his friend, and quieted down only when he received a letter from his friend Izyumchénko, who joyfully bore the same fate, and who expressed a firm conviction of the righteousness of his act.

(This friend was locked up in the guardhouse in Kursk for the same refusal to do military service. Just now, while I am writing these lines, this friend is kept in strictest secrecy, having no permission to see anyone in the Moscow transportation prison on his way to the Government of Tobólsk, to which he is being deported by order of the czar.)

And so, no matter how far we may personally stand from events of this character, we always involuntarily take part in them and influence them through our relation to them, or through our judgments of them.

Let us take the standpoint of his friend the revolutionist and consider that, to be able at some time, somewhere, to influence the external conditions of life, we can and must depart from the very first demands of our conscience, and we not only do not alleviate the sufferings and the struggle of men who strive to serve God, but we also prepare these sufferings of an inner discord for all those who will have to solve the dilemma in life. And there is not one who will not have to solve it. All of us, no matter how far we may be removed from such events, take part in them with our opinions and judgments. A thoughtless, careless word may become the source of the greatest sufferings for the best men in the world. We cannot be too careful in the use of this tool: "By your words you shall be justified, and by your words you shall be condemned."

But many of us are called to take part in such events not with words alone, but in a still more direct way. I am speaking of those who serve, who in one way or another take part in those hopeless oppressions, by means of which the government persecutes such men as Drózhzhin, and which only strengthen the movement. I am speaking of the participants in these persecutions, beginning with the emperor, the ministers, the judges, the prosecuting attorneys, and ending with the guards and jailers, who torture these martyrs. You all, participants in these torments, know that this man, whom you torture, is not only not a malefactor, but also an exceptionally good man; that he is being tormented for the very reason that he wants with all the forces of his heart to be good. You know that he is young, that he has friends and a mother, and that he loves you and forgives you. And you will put him in a lockup, will take away his clothes, starve him, not let him sleep, and deprive him of his communion with his neighbors and his friends.

How can you, emperor, who have signed such a decree, minister, prosecutor, superintendent of the prison, and jailer, sit down to your dinner knowing that he is lying on a cold floor, and in exhaustion is weeping on account of your malice? How can you caress your child? How can you think of God, or of death, which will lead you to Him? No matter how much you may pretend to be the executors of some invariable laws, you are simply men – good men. You are to be pitied, and you show pity, and only in this pity and love for one another does our life consist You say that necessity compels you to serve in your capacity. You know yourselves that that is not true. You know that there is no necessity, that necessity is a conventional word, that what for you is a necessity is for another a luxury. You know that you can find another position, one in which you will have no need to torture people – and what people! Precisely in this way did they torture the prophets, and later Christ, and later His disciples. Thus have they always tortured those who, loving them, lead them ahead to their good. If you could only refrain from being participants in these tortures!

It is terrible to torture an innocent bird or an animal. How much more terrible it is to torture a good, pure youth, who loves men and wishes them well. It is terrible to be a participant in this matter.

And, above all, to be a participant for nothing – to ruin his body, one's self, and one's soul, and yet not only not to put a stop to the consummation of the establishment of the kingdom of God, but, on the contrary, against one's will to contribute to its triumph.

It has come and is already here.

Moscow, March 4, 1895

——

Transcribed and edited by WWW.NONRESISTANCE.ORG.

This transcription is under no copyright protection. It is our gift to you.

You may freely copy, print, and transmit it, but please do not change or sell it.

And please bring any mistakes to our attention.

www.ingramcontent.com/pod-product-compliance
Lightning Source LLC
Chambersburg PA
CBHW021622290326
41931CB00047B/1420